Netiquette:

Modern Manners For A Modern World

The Ultimate Guide To Online Etiquette

NETIQUETTE: MODERN MANNERS FOR A MODERN WORLD

THE ULTIMATE GUIDE TO ONLINE ETIQUETTE

DR. NASRINE SHAH-ABUSHAKRA, PH.D

CONTENTS

Introduction:
Why Online Manners Matter

If you're over the age of thirty-five, you were likely not born with an iPhone in your hand as it seems new generations are. Texting, Skyping and Tweeting do not come as a second nature to you. You don't breathe social media, nor do you expect instant communication. In today's split-second-here-today-gone-in-an-instant news flashes and messaging society, your informal relationship with social media can be bad news. Ever-evolving technology has changed society as we know it, and if you don't know that, or only have a limited idea of what this means, this book is for you. The good news is that despite being part of a generation that has seen drastic changes with regard to communication and technology, most of us are at least familiar with social media, which has been a game-changer in nearly every aspect of how we go about our daily lives. The evolution of social media has drastically altered the landscape of personal and corporate lives today. Although the use of social media may not be intrinsic to the very being of our generation as it is for those in their teens and twenties who were born into this culture, our slightly more mature generation has been forced to learn quickly in order to survive and evolve. As older adults, we have an advantage over teens and twenty-somethings: we grew up in a time when good manners were instilled in us. Being polite is not a foreign concept to us. The manners that we use daily in face-to-face interactions are just as important in our online interactions.

I have written this book for you.

Read it, use it, and enjoy it, because I have been studying and using various social media for years. During my studies and usage of social media, I have also been more than perturbed at how casually rudeness, self-absorption and the general trampling of basic human courtesies have become on almost all social media, from Facebook to Twitter to texting. I grew up in a world where politeness and mindfulness mattered. We are now living in a world where new social media sites are being born every day. In this age of technology, it is easy to lose sight of the human side of our interactions, and good manners tend to go right out the window.

In *Netiquette*, I share my thoughts on how to combine the truly wonderful aspects of social media with the equally wonderful world of good manners and good taste.

It's a delightful combination.

People worldwide have used social media to start revolutions, link to long lost friends from years ago, find jobs, elect presidents, sing the songs of the unsung and make heroes. On the other hand, they have also used it to bully, cajole, embarrass, stalk, spread misinformation, and annoy others.

Never have more people been empowered. Never have more people been vulnerable and harassed.

We live in a world that didn't exist even one year ago, and each new day brings new technology along with faster, more efficient ways to communicate. These new tools and the millions of social media users worldwide who tap into them can literally start revolutions, change perspectives and open borders that had isolated cultures and minds for centuries.

But like every new advancement, from the automobile to the internet, the new social media can be abused. It can open not only frontiers and minds, but wide streams of unthinking, unsophisticated, and perhaps even unacceptable behavior. That is why I've written this book.

In my role as founder of the Al Wassla Group and most recently Dr. Nasrine, I've been internationally recognized as an ambassador between the Middle East and the Western World. I couldn't have gained that honor without being able to recognize, understand and use social media. I use it skillfully to connect with people—and I mean that in both the physical and the intellectual sense. I use it to bring these two worlds together elegantly, effectively, and in a way that acknowledges the brilliance and beauty of each culture.

I consider myself a true global citizen. I grew up in Boston's Back Bay and have since traveled the world—meeting with leaders such as President Clinton, Prime Minister Siniora of Lebanon, and HRH and Vice President of the UAE Mohammed bin Rashid Al Maktoum.

I serve on numerous committees dedicated to such causes as reviewing scholarly publications, family business, and promoting global understanding.

Technology has made my career possible. If we were still living in a world of letters, long-distance operator-supervised telephone calls, telegrams and telexes, nothing that I do now would have been remotely possible.

I believe that my experiences with social media, education, government and international affairs make me uniquely qualified to set worldwide standards for those who avail themselves of social media. (Hint: that's you.)

I hold a Master of Science in Information Systems and a Doctorate in Technology and Education. Throughout my educational career, I was a professor at the University of Michigan and also served as a Director of the Fulbright Teacher Exchange Orientation Program for the U.S. Department of State.

My personal history and circumstances have also highly influenced my interest in the evolution of social media. For example, my parents and grandparents hail from the Middle

East, and their generations tended to isolate and to identify people by their country of birth and culture.

Me? I'm a citizen of the world; a child of many cultures. I currently reside in both the Middle East and the U.S. and travel between the bustling, vibrant United Arab Emirates and Washington DC with frequency. While I grew up in Boston and obtained my formal education in the States, I've also gained immense knowledge from being a global citizen. I frequently travel the world, and am in daily contact with hundreds of people each day utilizing social media. You name a medium – Facebook, Twitter, Tumblr, blogs, Pinterest, LinkedIn, Skype, email – and I'm quite certain that you'll find me an avid and adoring user of it.

As I grew up, social media and the way that it is used evolved greatly. I am in an interesting position, straddled between a childhood wherein social media did not exist, and an adult, professional life wherein social media dominates my life. I became fascinated and entranced by the way social media allowed me to connect with the various cultures and friends that I've gained.

Thinking in terms of a global traveler, social media can be considered the passport that is available to all of us, despite our physical locations or cultural backgrounds. As with most creations and evolutions, I've found (as I'm sure you have) that the wonderful power of social media can become a weapon or hurtful tool if not used sensibly.

Nearly 100 years ago (prehistoric Stone Age times by comparison to today), a woman named Emily Post deemed herself the judge and jury of all things proper. She built quite a following for her societal advice, such as, "always write a thank you note," for a gift, a nice visit, or an extended invitation. Now we seem to be light years away from the time when a postage stamp and a letter allowed people to get in touch three or four days apart, and galaxies away from a time when even telephones were considered a luxury.

Is Ms. Post's advice applicable to social media users today? I suspect that younger generations would think not. Ms. Post's advice and knowledge could now be considered an old book, worn with time, a bit dusty, resting in a spot from which it hasn't moved in years on your grandparents' bookcase. However, Emily Post did write something all those years ago that does have some bearing on today's rapid-fire instant communication:

> "The letter you write, whether you realize it or not, is always a mirror which reflects your appearance, taste and character. A 'sloppy' letter with the writing all pouring into one corner of the page, badly worded, badly spelled, and with unmatched paper and envelope -- even possibly a blot-- proclaims the sort of person who would

have unkempt hair, unclean linen and broken shoe laces; just as a neat, precise, evenly written note portrays a person of like characteristics."

Nicely said, Emily. I couldn't agree more.

The way in which we communicate today, whether by text, tweet, email, Skype or on Facebook, LinkedIn, or Reddit, says volumes about ourselves, and an entirely new vocabulary has sprung up and continues to evolve nearly daily to fit within these media. Communication can be dehumanizing. Its very nature is ephemeral: here this instant, gone the next. This form of communication that allows users to never personally interact in person with others can lead to rude (and quite often appalling) behavior, misunderstandings, hurt feelings, misinterpretations, and bad judgment.

Take Facebook as just one example. More than 350 million people actively use this social network, meaning they log in daily to the site to read it, contribute to it, comment on it, and add to it with considerable frequency. If Facebook were a country, it would be the fifth largest country in the world, landing after China, India, the United States, and Indonesia.

Facebook is so powerful and so open that it has been banned in countries where free speech isn't a citizen's right, such as China, Syria, Vietnam, and Iran. It's so ubiquitous worldwide that it has been used to start revolutions in Tunisia and Egypt, as well as other places as part of the Arab Spring. And that's *just* Facebook. When you consider all of the other social media platforms, it can be overwhelming to consider their power within a global society.

In my own experience as an educator and consultant, I have seen and heard both the best and the worst of social media. Social media can open doors, open minds, and enlighten the world, but it can also be a boorish and cruel tool.

Read on to discover my input and suggested solutions regarding *Netiquette*, which I believe is a necessary element in teaching civilization and respect to make the world of social media an existence of utopian ideals.

I. The History of Netiquette: Employing Elegance

There is no question that people often post rude, thoughtless messages on social media. However, have you ever asked yourself how and when this phenomena began? This is a question that plagues me. How can we objectively identify a particular message or trend as rude or inappropriate? While there are certainly some specific guidelines to follow, a good general rule of thumb is that you'll know it when you see it.

Social media refashions itself very quickly as it grows and as more people use it. New habits and new rules can quite literally change from day to day. Contemporary tools and capabilities within social media have created many standards, some that I believe are quite good and beneficial, and others that, frankly, I find odious.

Social media changes quickly, but people, on the other hand, are not so quick to change. That's part of the problem; we might be rude and not even be aware of it. Different social media platforms tend to have different languages and nuances within them. Further muddying these waters is the fact that users of social media may actually be unaware of their inappropriateness.

At worst, users may be fully aware of their inappropriate comments and choose to intentionally use social media as a tool to bring harm and hurt to others.

The internet and social media are like a mob-ruled society. Given the rapid exchange of information, the ease at which this information can be exchanged, and the number of users on social media, there seems to be an intrinsic belief that because others are acting poorly, it's quite alright to engage and interact with negativity and hostility en masse.

Most older adults who use social media think of Facebook as the dominant source for social media.

However, Facebook is actually going through massive internal changes and platform modifications in order to remain relevant. Facebook has reached the point where its popularity has made it unpopular. Now that their parents and even grandparents are on Facebook, teens and twenty-somethings don't want to be a part of it anymore.

If you have spent much time on Facebook at all, you can probably identify with those people who collect Facebook friends as if it were a high school popularity contest. Given the vague definitions of privacy within Facebook, this act of amassing thousands of "friends" could and should be greatly weighted. In many cases, I think, most of these "friends" barely know the collector. What is the point of adding a friend whom you barely know?

What does that say about the communication and interaction among "friends" on the network?

Spending much time on social media can even bring about a negative impact on a person's mental health. Users report feeling worthless and anxious after engaging with the Facebook platform. Most of our Facebook friends tend to share only the happiest and most appealing moments of their lives. This leaves others to wonder why their lives don't seem to compare, and why they don't also lead lives of seeming perfection and bliss.

Another Facebook faux pas is sending a message that requires the recipient to install an app in order to read a message, such as, "Ed has sent you an anniversary greeting. Install Happy Anniversary to view the content." Given the massive amounts of personal data that is gleaned and stored by corporations when you accept these invitations, one would be wise to pause and reflect on why you should utilize the

suggested app or platform to begin with.

Sadly, the art form of the written word is dwindling. Is it

really necessary to install layers upon layers of social media to

communicate? For example, Facebook Messenger is an app

that you must separately download onto your phone in order to

be able to send messages back and forth on Facebook from

your mobile device, despite the fact that you already have the

Facebook application installed on your device.

Most Facebook users can name a few friends who

gleefully share every time they have given a life on Candy

Crush Saga, or name the friend of a friend who sends dozens of

bad and bland, truly unfunny or offensive jokes every day.

Seeing these items pop up in your Facebook news feed can feel

like nails running down a chalkboard or the incessant blaring of

a car alarm.

Then there always seems to be the friend who apparently has so much free time that they are compelled to provide hourly updates on even the most mundane of details of their lives, from housework accomplished to what food has been consumed on a daily basis.

Lastly, if you choose to share your ardently held political views on Facebook, you must be prepared for others to disagree with them. Facebook provides a forum that virtually guarantees a wide range of disparate opinions. The discussion of politics and points of view in a social forum provides users with the opportunity to intelligently and articulately express opinions. However, it does not give anyone the right to be rude or dismissive of opposing views. Go ahead and express your political and personal opinions in a respectful and diplomatic manner, but keep in mind that it is best to stick to the old adage, "if you can't say anything nice, don't say anything at all."

The automatic responses that you receive once you do "follow" someone on social media, like direct messages (DMs) on Twitter, may seem personal, but are actually far from it. Thanks to the proliferation of "Like" and "retweet" buttons, users can – and often do – share content without actually having read it. This is far from useful, and it sends a message that your interactions are unimportant and meaningless.

These instances are not major faux pas; they are merely irritants. Such behavior is the equivalent in Emily Post's days of eating with one's elbows on the table.

What I've grown to believe and profess after years of teaching and using social media, is that a sensible, *human* set of rules for which people should be responsible should apply. Just as bad habits can proliferate on social media sites, good, sensible, dare I say *polite,* commonly accepted rules can proliferate there, as well.

At the core of this belief is the importance of reminding readers to be considerate of other people's feelings, know how people use the various social media sites, know where you are within your own personal and moral system, respect others people's space and thoughts, share your knowledge when appropriate, and be polite when someone errs.

Is it acceptable to send a sympathy note through someone's Facebook page? Break off a relationship with a text message? Fire someone with a tweet? We'll cover all of these scenarios and much more in later chapters.

Buddhists practice the concept of mindfulness, which is a state of active, open attention on the present. When you're mindful, you observe your thoughts and feelings from a distance, without judging them as good or bad. Instead of letting your life pass you by, mindfulness means living in the moment and awakening to experience.

In terms of netiquette in the social media, I would take this wonderful concept—a concept that promotes serenity and understanding—and mold it a bit to say this: Be aware of who will read your message. Be aware of when they will be reading it and how it will affect them. Be aware of and respectful of someone's privacy, and be aware of the power of what you hold in your hands.

Take the case of Mohamed Bouazizi, for example. A 26-year-old Tunisian fruit and vegetable seller, he was literally the spark that set off the Arab Spring in 2011. He was the sole support for his mother and his seven siblings, and was humiliated and abused by a policewoman in the Tunisian town of Sidi Bouzid. She confiscated the fruit and vegetable cart with which he made his living. Bouazizi set himself on fire in front of the local government building. Fatally burned, he lingered in agony for more than two weeks as immense anger mounted within and around Tunisia, fed by Facebook and other social media outcries of injustice. When Bouazizi died, the authoritarian government of President Zine el Abidine Ben Ali found itself with merely ten days to survive as the first of the revolutions to rock the region sent the dictator fleeing.

Consider just these few Facebook facts below, which demonstrate the power and influence of social media. In addition to Facebook, users access a plethora of social media sites, including Twitter, Google+, Pinterest, StumbleUpon, Reddit, Tumblr, and so many more.

- Facebook has more than 350 million active users, and 35 million people update their status each day.

- More than 2.5 billion pictures are uploaded on Facebook each month.

- The average Facebook user has 130 friends and sends eight friend requests each month.

- A recent survey of 500 top colleges in the US found that ten percent of admissions officers acknowledged looking at social networking sites such as Facebook to evaluate applicants.

- Americans spend roughly 13.9 billion (*that's billion with a B*) on Facebook and five billion on MySpace.

- If Facebook were a country, it would be the fifth largest country in the world, after China, India, the United States, and Indonesia.

Then consider these examples, which demonstrate how social media sites can be intrusive or abusive:

- An 18-year-old Wisconsin man posed as several different girls on Facebook to blackmail underage male teens into performing sexual favors by coaxing them to send nude photos of themselves. He could be facing up to 300 years in prison.

- Beacon, part of Facebook's controversial advertisement system that broadcast information about a user's shopping activity on other sites, was the target of a class action lawsuit in 2009. The resulting settlement required Facebook to pay $9.5 million into a group fund.

Let us not forget about Big Brother. It could be convincingly argued that we are indeed living in an Orwellian reality where our governments are prying into our deepest and most personal thoughts.

In the spring of 2013, *The Washington Post*, using a top-secret document it had obtained, revealed that the US National Security Agency (NSA) and the FBI had been tapping directly into the servers of nine leading US internet companies, extracting audio and video chats, photographs, emails, and other documents without user knowledge or consent. According to this top-secret document, information was collected directly from the servers of Microsoft, Google, Yahoo, Facebook, PalTalk, AOL, Skype, YouTube, and Apple.

I mention this not as any sort of political statement, but as an illustration of the power and sheer number of people who avail themselves of social media. If you are sharing your personal thoughts, ideas and concepts within social media platforms believing that you have the right to privacy with regard to your messages and data use, keep in mind that it has been clearly demonstrated that governments are both very aware of how much of your information is on these various sites, and that they are quite capable of accessing that information without your knowledge or direct consent.

Just think of the incredible power that these social media platforms place in both your hands and the hands of your government.

So where do we go from here? Where do we look to find an elegant and thoughtful solution? How do we refine our own habits to engage in meaningful and considerate dialogue? How do we put "social" back into the social media?

Throughout my own unique journeys around the world, I have always had an evolving concept of the definition of the word "culture". I believe this open-mindedness has helped me transcend many stereotypes and societal norms in order to form a global perception of the word. From the days of my youth, I've been exposed to Eastern culture and Western culture, which were the worlds of my parents and grandparents. I'm also from the in-between generations of A and Y cultures. I'm a third-culture kid, an adult and a woman. I am part of a global nation, and I am part of cultural assimilation. These compilations of so many layers have molded me into the advocate of social media civility and elegance that I am today.

Consider this basic definition of culture:

cul·ture 1. *the quality in a person or society that arises from a concern for what is regarded as excellent in arts, letters,* *manners, scholarly pursuits, etc. 2. that which is excellent in*

the arts, manners, etc. 3. a particular form or stage of

civilization, as that of a certain nation or period: Greek

culture. 4. developments or improvement of the mind by

education or training. 5. the behaviors and beliefs

characteristic of a particular social, ethnic, or age group: the

social media culture.

If we blend the above definition and apply it to our

modern times, it is painfully obvious that we are caught in a

shift—maybe even a revolution—of "culture" as we know it

and the generations prior to us have known it.

Previously, Emily Post would insist that it was proper

manners for one to compose a thank-you note for various

occasions in a timely manner.

Today, we wield technology and email our gratitude instead (if at all). It isn't a rarity to see "thank you" and "happy birthday" shared on social media rather than spoken between friends today. Emily Post stood for taste, class and refinement. When did those go out of style? Why can't we apply the same standards 100 years later?

I think we can.

When many of us are online or living in a virtual world, we in a way define that word. We use the new media in such a way that it sometimes literally becomes our social landscape. We can and do define it as we see fit.

A dear friend once explained, "It's as if I walk into a club; of course I walk over to the different tables and say hello. I chat with my artist friends. I move on to my grammar school friends, my college and graduate school peers and friends. Then there are my friends from my career, so I say hello to them and then I move on to...." This is the way we navigate our lives online today, and it's not uncommon.

Understanding the complexity and diversity of this virtual world on endless levels makes it challenging to focus on simply one medium within the arena of social media, just as it was difficult for my friend to speak the same way to very different groups of her friends.

Social media has become vast and all-encompassing. The cultural landscape of how we interact and who we are online within the boundaries of social media platforms has taken on a unique structure. Geography no longer applies to physical landscapes throughout the globe, but rather is denoted, by age, income, education and professional careers in common.

Take, for example, a study by *The Guardian*, a UK newspaper, that found that the average 12- to 15-year-old has never met one in four of their "friends" on social networking sites such as Facebook. Yet these young people earnestly believe that these "friends" are indeed friends. They share their most personal details of their lives with people who are, in essence, complete strangers.

There is no denying that social media has united many people and formed deep bonds that have allowed individuals to grow and feel less alone in the world, and that is powerful indeed. But we must establish a strong foundation in order to render that wonderful kinship in a positive, elegant, and promising manner.

II. Do Not Disturb: Mobile Manners in Public Places

In later chapters we'll cover all of the facets of acceptable, polite, and refined use of social media, from business to academic to public and private exchanges, from why saying something snarky and funny in quick text to a friend is perfectly fine, but saying the same thing to a boss in an email isn't. In many instances what is polite and acceptable is dictated by who you are communicating with. Personal and professional rules and standards vary, as well they should.

This chapter will focus on what is perhaps the most curious and complex blending of your public and personal selves.

How many times have you been visiting with a friend or two over coffee or dinner, trying to engage in a great conversation while their iPhone sits in the middle of the table like an uninvited, boorish, and irritating guest? While you're talking, the phone seems to hold the attention of your friend constantly, whether it's beeping or not. How many times during conversations have you had to quit speaking entirely to wait for your companion to text or speak to some unseen person on the other end? Suddenly, you have become the invisible force and suddenly *you* feel like the uninvited guest.

To me, there is little doubt what these actions convey: whoever is on the other end of the conversation or text is more important than the person sharing the actual physical space. These days you can see this sort of situation nearly everywhere: People who are out together sharing social interactions are actually very far apart, focused more on the image that they project online versus the quality of their real-life interactions, separated by their addiction to the constant contact of mobile devices.

A "social" media? There is nothing social about these far too common situations.

As media like Twitter, Facebook, Tumblr, LinkedIn, Instagram, Vine, Snapchat, Google+, texts and other online arenas have made it easier and faster to communicate, they have also made rudeness far more common. This is not acceptable. A social and engaging community relies upon the fundamental skills of consideration and genuine interaction.

As the number of portable devices and social platforms increases, so too does the chance that you will become an equal-opportunity offender. You may very well find yourself to be the person others will be staring at on the train or in the restaurant because you are engaging in conversations that aren't visible. You may become the subject of eye-rolls and deep sighs without even recognizing it.

As I write this, there are by some estimates close to 7 million iPhones in use in the United States right now. And with only the slightest exaggeration, by the time I finish writing this paragraph, there will be 10,000 more. Given the astronomical growth of these ubiquitous pieces of equipment, the number of handheld and portable devices that allow instant access to the rest of the world will no doubt keep climbing. Mind boggling when you think about it, isn't it?

What does that mean in our quest for civility and sensibility in today's world of instant and constant communication?

Here is the crux of social media engagement in a nutshell: Turning to your smartphone and away from colleagues in business meetings or diverting your attention from teachers, lecturers, artists, performers or your own family and friends is simply rude and disrespectful.

Interrupting conversations around you in social settings, including public transportation, waiting rooms, grocery stores, restaurants, theaters or anywhere people congregate while you talk loudly or text madly on your smartphone is boorish.

The phenomenon of social media has opened a completely new universe of communications. You can literally talk, text or email anyone, anywhere and anytime. You can post to social media and connect with vast audiences at any given time. Is this a positive advancement for the betterment of communication and global awareness? Or does this new technology open a Pandora's box of societal ills, giving everyone the right to annoy and offend at any time?

It all depends. Where are you using social media? How are you using it? To whom are you communicating? When are you communicating?

The fact that there are any number of apps available to help users be more subtle and less irritating in public – on trains, planes or busses or in crowded public spaces – speaks for itself. There is a great demand for these apps, and manufacturers have recognized the urgency for less intrusive means of communication within public forums and have moved quickly to appease these desires.

The standard and oft-cited annoyance of talking loudly on your cell on the train or subway or in a crowded room as if you're invisible and silent is fairly easy to deem as socially unacceptable. It is rude, inconsiderate, and offensive. Simply put, reverse Nike's well-known mantra, and don't do it. But verbally communicating loudly within public confines is an easily defined faux pas. What about more subtle cases of social interaction? When *is* it appropriate to tap into your iPhone and work or chat to catch up with friends?

The first rule—and this applies not just to public use, but all of the time in all circumstances: Respect other people's presence and time. Being on a train or plane or anywhere that you find yourself surrounded by others, demands that you be aware of how your behavior is affecting others. Are you talking too loudly? Are you not paying attention to the words being spoken to you? Are you totally oblivious to the conductor, flight attendant or cashier trying to get your attention?

What we call "communication" today has quite nearly taken over every waking moment of our lives, and, as with any all-consuming issue, this is not necessarily a good thing. If we are constantly at the mercy of our mobile devices or online personas, we're actually not doing anyone any good. We are never really 100% present within any moment. And if we are in public, surrounded by hundreds of people and focused only on our devices, we are first being incredibly antisocial, and secondly, just plain rude. We are not conducting ourselves with even the most basic pretenses of civil good, such as holding doors for others, or simply acknowledging their existence.

The ability to be constantly tied to your desk or office doesn't improve your level of work, since you're easily distracted or not focused on one task at a time. When you think about it, genuine social mindfulness is tossed aside for the *appearance* of social attentiveness. There is a very clear distinction between these two qualities, and they are bound to have long-lasting effects upon generations to come.

While all of us—and, yes, that includes me—are likely addicted to smartphone or online technology, given its powerful magnetic pulls on us, we don't have to abandon our manners or basic decency. Think about this for a moment: Do you text while you're out socially, on a date, in a meeting, at the dinner table, or, God forbid, while you're driving somewhere?

If you answered those questions honestly and said yes more than no, you are most likely driving people around you crazy with your inattention. And make no mistake, there is a good reason for their unhappiness.

A recent magazine article that I read focused on the topic of public smartphone use and pointed to examples of people using their phones to send messages during funerals. How many times can you recall attending a performance or event that calls for attention and heard a cell phone begin buzzing or ringing to the dismay of the audience? Probably many. A survey in the UK found that people would rather watch someone committing the rather foul social ill of picking their nose than experiencing an oblivious cell-phone user assaulting the space around them. Think of the idea of having a private bubble, and recognize that those private bubbles are not sound-proof.

Each member of polite society must demonstrate consideration of others in order to assure a world where manners and human interactions are genuine. I admit that these noted articles are extreme examples of social unawareness, but they demonstrate our shared annoyance levels regarding communication that have sky-rocketed throughout the world.

There has actually been some movement in certain areas to enact laws that would ban the use of smartphones and other like devices in public when there is an increased likelihood of danger to others caused by the distraction, such as texting and driving. While these laws are laudable, I believe that they would be nearly impossible to enforce. Consider how many people you still see texting and driving; this is emblematic of our need for constant social interaction and the backlash against any limitation thereof.

In addition to legal maneuvers by government officials to curb the usage of smartphones and technology, there is also a social revolution on the rise regarding the rudeness and inconsideration of using these devices in public spaces. In most cases, it's not looked upon with great favor by others should you grab your smartphone in the middle of a movie to tweet or update your Facebook status. Chances are, the people seated around you are going to be tossing a few snotty looks and possibly harsh words in your direction. What if you actually answer your phone during the movie? More than likely, you are going to be tossed out to a round of great applause by fellow audience members.

Here I note another anomaly via yet another survey—this one conducted on behalf of a film industry trade magazine. The survey suggests that while the above-mentioned activities are worthy of disdain, there is also an undercurrent of them conversely growing more acceptable. 55% of those surveyed admitted to texting during a movie, and 27% admitted that they had checked their Facebook status during a movie.

The survey reported that "A majority of 18-to-34-year-olds polled believe using social media while watching a movie in a theater would add to their experience, and nearly half would be interested in going to theaters that allowed texting and web surfing."

Things are changing, that is for certain; the old adage is true: the only constant is change.

One thing I do know with certainty is this: people are more likely to be rude on social media than in person. I spend a great deal of time in airplanes and airports because of family and business commitments. I love traveling immensely, and genuinely enjoy striding back and forth between the

Middle East and the US because it keeps my cultural instincts sharp and my awareness of basic human interaction keen, no matter what culture I happen to be living in at the moment.

I have had countless opportunities to see the proof of that statement in action. Place a laptop, iPhone or an iPad in someone's hands, and they do things they normally would not do, like ignore others or talk loudly. I've found in my research that as social media usage soars, so has incivility, with many people reporting that they have no qualms about being less polite when locked into their smartphone.

I would like to make an effort to keep the "social" in social media. Think of it this way: Much like the Hippocratic Oath taken by physicians that dictated, "First, Do No Harm," all users of social media should take the own, slight adapted oath: "First, Do Not Annoy."

Take a look at just a few of these recent examples: in Wisconsin, a county supervisor stopped a meeting and told public participants to stop texting and tweeting, or they would be escorted out of the building. In a Pennsylvania courtroom, a judge admonished a member of the gallery for texting during traffic court and suggested that he would have the bailiff remove her.

These outcries against the public use of such things as tweets, blogs and texting are not confined to the U.S. In Quebec, the use by the public, lawyers and journalists of texts and online blogs during court hearings was banned in order to "ostensibly to maintain decorum and order in Quebec courts."

"It is prohibited to broadcast or communicate text messages, observations, information, notes, photographs, audio or video recordings from inside the courtroom to the outside," reads the directive, which will apply to hearings in Quebec

Court, Superior Court and the Quebec Court of Appeal, the ruling stated.

In Australia, a bill was proposed that would ban electronic devices in courtrooms and levy a fine of $2,300 and 12-month prison term on anyone found sharing information about a case privately or on social media.

But the point is--people have always been very interested in relaying information, whether it's a chat with friends or late-breaking news in a courtroom. Now they have the ability to do so at any time.

And as you can see, there is a growing backlash to this public practice of what should be a private exercise. Will users eventually self-enforce? Will they at some point establish unwritten rules? That is unlikely, I think, which is why I've written this book.

Remember what your life was like before smartphones and all the social media you could connect them to? It seems like years ago to me, but I sort of remember it as a time when I was having so much fun being with my friends and talking to them in person that I didn't need to be plugged in constantly.

It was an almost serene way of life, without the constant electronic interruption.

I think in today's world, where smartphones and public use of them are not going away, that a few small applications of commonsense and down home courtesy will go a very long way in bringing serenity to today's plugged-in world.

Things seem to have evolved to the point where we have created a society where the things I've discussed in this chapter —the isolated and almost constant public use of today's instant communications technology—have become so acceptable that we need a loud and strident wake-up call.

We have created a society of "connected" and insensitive boors. We need mindfulness and sensitivity and, as I've said before— elegance and refinement.

III. You Are What You Post

The entire idea of social media is sharing – information, ideas, tips, opinions, and advice. But how you do so, and who you share it with, makes all the difference in the world in how successful you are.

Your ability to connect on the many social media outlets depends on many things. The first, of course, is what you are using, because each text, Reddit, tweet, email, Skype, Facebook share, or LinkedIn comment has its own subtle and not-so-subtle differences. But no matter what you're using to communicate, or who and why you're trying to reach them, it's not your intelligence, or your forcefulness, or even your writing skills that matter.

Yes, all these are important. Of course they are. But the one thing that truly matters--just as in real life-- is your online personality. It works just like it does in real life. You choose people to hang out with because of interests, hobbies, and style. And the opposite is true, as well. You identify others you meet —and usually very quickly—as people you want to avoid like the plague. Just as in real life, there are people who you'd prefer to avoid. In fact, you run the other way if you saw them on the street. Who wants to be bored or grossed out or simply numbed by silly or obnoxious or offensive conversations? It's just unappealing.

The same is true online. It works the same way on social media.

We'll talk here about some sensibilities and rules for making the most of your time online, and how to avoid the embarrassing mistakes that will have people running away from your tweets or posts or texts or Facebook requests.

I'm going to throw this out here, because I just received this notification from someone I barely know on Facebook. This person, whose identity I will protect for reasons that will become clear after you read the post below, is actually a friend of a friend I somehow became connected with.

Here is what I recently received as a Facebook post:

Hello to all of you who are on my list of contacts of Facebook. I haven't wanted to do this, but after finding photos located on another site, I would like to ask a favor of you just for a little privacy for us all. You may not know that Facebook has changed its privacy configuration once again. Thanks to the new "Graphic app", any person on FB anywhere in the world can see our photos, our "likes" and our "comments."
During the next two weeks, I am going to keep this message posted and I ask you to do the following and

comment "DONE." Please do this, because I want the

information I share with you, my friends, to remain

among my friends and not be available to the whole

world. I want to be able to publish photos of my friends

and family without strangers being able to see them,

which is what happens now when you choose "like" or

"comment." Unfortunately we cannot change this

configuration because FB has made it like this.

1. So, please, place your cursor over my photo that

appears in this box (without clicking) and a window will

open.

2. Now move the cursor to the word "Friends", again

without clicking and then on "Settings".

3. Un-check "Life Events" and "Comments and Like".

This way my activity with my family and friends will no

longer be made public.

4. Now, copy and paste this text on your own wall (do

not "share" it!). Once I see it published on your page, I

will uncheck the same

Thank you!

I did not make this up, nor did I massage this message to

make a point here. I'm not kidding. Is this someone who might

have a little too much time on his hands? Is this someone who

might assume we all have just as much idle time on our hands

as he apparently does? How many recipients of this Facebook

post do you think will follow this laborious instruction? And to

what end?

This is just one type of social media behavior that is sure

to lead to a lonely existence. But it is not the only one. As I

have said, "You are what you post," and in this case, it was

annoying.

Here is my rule Number One: Be mindful of how even the smallest message will affect others. But this insensitivity is not the only type of egregious behavior that will shape how others view you through your posts or tweets.

Remember, it is impossible to appeal to everyone you contact. Human nature creates varied personalities and makes it certain that no matter how witty or entertaining or knowledgeable or helpful you might think you are, someone somewhere is not going to like you. But you do want to appeal to someone, maybe many. And you can if you are aware how you might be affecting others with your messages.

This next section will strike you—at least I hope it will strike you—as entirely negative. I happen to think that negativity is easier to slip into than positivity. It takes less energy to criticize and knock someone down—to be snide and snotty and entirely critical. And I apologize for it, because that is not my nature and that is not the purpose of this book.

But I think in this instance, it is important to outline some of the various annoying personalities out there right now on the social media. Think about some of these types of people. I think they are common enough on the various social media for you to recognize them. Just don't recognize them in yourself, or if you do, change your habits. Immediately.

The Dementors: The German's have the concept of *schadenfreude*, which is defined as, "delighting in others' misfortune"—the idea that when people around us have bad luck, we look better to ourselves. Some researchers have found that people with low self-esteem are more likely to feel *schadenfreude* than are people who have high self-esteem.

J.K. Rowling, in her incredibly popular Harry Potter series, created Dementors, dark creatures who feed off of human happiness. In other words, the Dementors seek out happy humans and suck away whatever is positive, thus causing depression and despair. Some people call these types Energy Vampires.

There are people all around us who bring joy and lightness into our lives, sometimes unexpectedly. You can almost reach out and touch their energy. Then there are others who can leave us feeling totally whacked out and stressed, maybe even guilty about some undefined things we didn't even do.

You might know someone who is an eternal victim, always suffering because of some perceived wrong, or someone who constantly feels the world is totally against them.

Or the people who need to always be the center of attention, or those who wallow in blaming everyone but themselves, or the drama queen, who can make a burned-out light bulb an international crisis.

If my first rule is to be mindful, my second rule is to not use social media to expound or otherwise whine or complain or put people down. Briefly are some other types:

The center of the universe: The types are pretty easy to spot. You'll discover them bragging about their achievements. Even worse, they seem to enjoy re-tweeting compliments about themselves so the whole wide world can know how wonderful they are and they enjoy talking much more than listening. Remember that no one like a blowhard. Make your social media experience a conversation instead of a one-way monologue.

The smarmy sales guy: These are the types who love to hit you hard and often with steady streams of promotional messages. All offers, all the time. You know them: "Thanks for following! Check out my blog! Like me on Facebook! Download my e-book!" They are really the new spammers of the social web. And it is almost always one-way. And eventually they will be shut off.

Silent Sam: When you were younger, say in high school or even junior high, you never really paid too much attention to the quiet girl in the corner. It is the same on social media. Be respectful of the time of others, but please don't be quiet. No one will know you're out there. What's the point of using social media if that is the case? Join in and encourage other to do so as well.

There are many other types, but you get the point: There are users of social media who stand out not for their likability but rather for their annoyances.

Now comes the positive part, the reason why I wrote this book. Here I hope is advice you can use to make the most of your social media experience. Life is short, so share your joy.

Don't be selfish: What makes social media unique is the ability to develop relationships with people you wouldn't have had the opportunity to meet otherwise. So, strike up a conversation and get to know some of the people around you. Wonderful things happen when you do. Share stories you like, and like the comments on your friends' news feeds and support them in what they are trying to do. Chances are they will do the same thing for you. Build them up. Share their stuff. Retweet their posts.

Be helpful: And entertaining and funny and inspiring, or clever. Be friendly and be modest. Done tastefully and consistently, I can almost guarantee your content will be shared and your network will grow. Remember that personalities build relationships—good personalities, that is. Don't be shy about sharing what you know and trying to help people by pointing them in the right direction. When offering advice to others, remember that it is usually better to say "This is what worked for me . . ." than to dictate "This is what you need to do . . ." Focus on helping other people solve their problems instead of focusing on yourself.

Participate: Ask and answer questions, join conversations and groups, comment on others' updates, retweet, etc. Share your accomplishments, articles you've written, professional challenges you've overcome (but as I wrote earlier, don't come across as a blowhard; it's a fine line.)

Invite people to share, comment, like, re-tweet, sign up for your newsletter, visit your website or whatever you want them to do. It doesn't hurt to check in from time to time with your social media contacts and see how they are, like their statuses, wish them happy birthday, ask their opinion.

I'll close this chapter with some simple and easy to apply suggestions that will help you hone your online personality, to draw people to you rather than pushing them away from you.

First and foremost, remember whom you are talking to. On Facebook, for example, you are sharing information with everyone that you have added as a friend, if not the entire world. Be very aware of the constantly updated Facebook privacy policies. Facebook previously set all of your posts and updates to public status, but then backed down after a great public outcry.

You can create groups and lists on Facebook that allow you to choose who you share things with, but remember, if your friends don't have their settings locked down, you could be sharing with others that the posts aren't meant for.

On Twitter you are sharing information with everyone, period, unless you have a locked or private account. Private accounts allow only your followers to see what you post and what you reply to others, however, they also tend to defeat the purpose of Twitter, which was designed to be a fast-moving and public forum that can be tailored to any subject matter that you could possibly be interested in. Twitter is a public network. (Be sure you completely understand; again, I stress the importance of understanding the privacy settings. While it can be confusing and time-consuming to read through them, having a firm grasp on this knowledge can prevent many an embarrassing moment on any social network.)

Speaking of embarrassment, always proofread your posts. Definitely don't rely too much on spellcheck; we've all seen entire websites dedicated to spellcheck fails or changes that are mortifying at best. Spellcheck doesn't prevent you from using the wrong word or wrong form of a word. Pay close attention to what you have written.

Earlier I wrote about being mindful of how you are perceived. This means always remembering that you are sharing in a very public place when you are part of a social media platform. Don't share too much information on personal matters like quarrels with friends or significant others, photos of your children that could be embarrassing, etc. And please, please remember that not everyone has the same sense of humor. Err on the side of sensitivity with your jokes and comments. What you might think is hilariously funny, others might deem obnoxious.

IV. THE EVOLUTION OF CULTURAL STANDARDS

Let's say for argument's sake that you are bursting with things you want to share and you walk into a room. In the room you see some friends, but most of the large group is strangers listening to music and talking quietly amongst themselves. And let's say that since your friends know you and your eccentricities, they might be willing to accept the fact that you jump up on a chair and start yelling your news. They might not even mind all that much if you interrupt conversations, just butting right in before others can finish their sentences or thoughts. Maybe you even turn off the music and start banging some pots and pans together. Now you're starting to annoy even your closest friends who accept your eccentricities--and the strangers want you to shut up. Actually, they probably want you to leave.

In that scenario, your behavior has become unacceptable. Who sets the rules for group behavior? Some of it is common sense, at least in a public forum such as the gathering I imagined above. In such a case you don't scream or bang pots and pans or take off your clothes or shut off the music or interrupt conversations.

What about online in the social media? How do you when jumping on a soapbox is acceptable versus standing politely making small talk? As the various media expands and matures, users are maturing and adapting, as well. Some of those adaptations have led to being more aware of others and respecting varying opinions and viewpoints. Unfortunately, some of those adaptations have let to "trolls"; vile individuals who seek to cause embarrassment and threaten harm to others while veiled in a cloak of anonymity.

How exactly do we define social media? According to the more academic definition of social media, it is "a group of Internet-based applications that build on the ideological and technological foundations that allow the creation and exchange of user-generated content."

That's a great statement once you take the time to break it down, but it is quite a mouthful. This definition is rather sterile and complex, so I'd like to qualify and humanize it a bit.

Let's face it, people still obtain their information from a variety of sources derived from the old-fashioned media like radio, television and newspapers, but the online world has drastically changed the news cycles and printing industry. Social media is different from the traditional media because they are relatively inexpensive, always accessible, and completely owner-driven. You, the user, are in absolute and total control of which stories you choose to read.

Media moguls and conglomerates in the news industry have struggled to try to keep up with the rapid changes of this ever-evolving online world. As opposed to simply reading a newspaper, listening to a radio report, or watching the nightly television news, you can now easily select when you obtain your news and how you obtain it.

Media outlets are hyper-aware of the importance of social media presences that are compelled to draw readers into their links or articles, and the press now never goes to sleep. There is no "we've gone to print" in this digital age. The internet has transformed the news cycle into a 24/7 social media revolution; a wheel that is always turning.

While this evolution has let to greater global awareness and wisdom, it can also be frightening.

The social media and the technologies around which they operate are presented in a vast variety of forms and forums: e-mags, internet chat rooms, weblogs, social blogs, microblogs, Instagram, idea-sharing sites like Pinterest and Tumblr…the list goes on and on and on. How many tech startups have you heard about within the last month alone? All of this aside, in its simplest and most practical of terms, we use social media to stay in contact with the world around us.

These media are different, and yet they are also the same. The various social media sites share a common goal: uniting people in global communities. I live in the Middle East, but I can share and talk and laugh and interact with my friends and colleagues in Boston, Washington DC and around the globe with great alacrity. I know what's going on with my friends as if I were living next door; I get to hear all about family news, educational trends, business ideas, new tips for childcare, and funny stories.

So how do you choose how and what to share? What are the standards and rules for doing so? The term "social media" refers to what platform we use and the means we use to craft, share and exchange information. Where we choose to share that information, what virtual communities we are part of, and what networks we inhabit create our online beings.

Academicians would furthermore point out, according to one Wikipedia entry, "that media depends on mobile and web-based technologies to create highly interactive platforms through which individuals and communities share, co-create, discuss, and modify user-generated content. It introduces substantial and pervasive changes to communication between organizations, communities, and individuals."

While Wikipedia is a wonderful resource dedicated to providing knowledge of nearly any topic to a global audience, I'm not about sterile academic entries. I am really and truly about understanding and conveying a common thread of decency, courtesy and politeness for all the various social media. I want to establish a common language for what at times is a Tower of Babel (or perhaps, even more pointedly, a Tower of Babble, of hierarchy of chaos, misuse and obnoxious behavior) for users. My goal regarding netiquette is to establish easily understood rules for any various social media platforms.

Years ago, in my old stomping grounds of Boston, a judge was asked to define pornography. Paraphrased, his response was that he actually couldn't come up with a specific all-encompassing definition. But, he added, "I know it when I see it." That's how I feel about inappropriate online behavior. I would like to reach a point where users don't need a detailed, prescriptive list of what is wrong or unacceptable use of social media. I would like to reach a point where users will simply know it when they see it.

If you use a certain medium for sharing, you know the basic rule and the particular specifics of how and why and where and when. If you have studied and read and participated in various forums on various sites, you've probably not done so to establish a "how to" guidebook or a manual for users, which is what I had in mind when I wrote this book. What I was looking for was a common thread of behavior that is acceptable for users, beyond which in any online community you would be ostracized or banned or otherwise not welcome.

Let's take a look at some of the explicit rules for various sites and see if we can intuit some sense of general rules for proper behavior.

Google+: According to its website, Google+ netiquette is the "cultural code users follow when using the Google+ social network." I start with them because the rules of Google+ "are the most strict social networking rules in the industry because Google programming code is strict. Google has the best programs in all of internet programming. Their programming skills have led to a monopoly position in many markets because other companies code inferior products. The superior code of Google has given the company a place of trust in the mind of consumers."

Well, so much for modesty. Nonetheless, Google+ does make one statement worth noting. Its rules for netiquette, it states, are centered around how one might act in reality, because your Google+ account is tied to reality. In its simplest terms, Google's mantra is "do no evil," which I support wholeheartedly.

YouTube: A recent blog on the use of YouTube and its perceived rules, which like all the various rules evolved over time, stated among others things that YouTubers should not, despite a feeling that sometimes anything goes, post videos that: are pornographic or sexually explicit; contain frontal nudity; feature graphic violence; include disturbing or disgusting video footage; violate copyright laws; contain hate speech, including verbal attacks based on gender, sexual orientation, race, ethnicity, religion, disability or nationality; or, finally, reveal other users' personal information.

This informative and clear posting was followed by a string of comments on a contributor's website discussing various rules he had set out and recommended. The best comments of the lot—and these comments were from users all around the world – came from a reader in Finland who seemed to end the various discussions with a very concise summary: "Don't be an asshole." Is that a universal concept? I think so.

Twitter: Let's take a look at some of the rules of behavior for Twitter. Here are two definitions that perhaps sum it all up, much like the Google mantra above:

Twanker:- *An egocentric individual, celebrity or organization who uses Twitter only for one-way broadcasting about their own greatness.*

Twidiot : *An individual or organization that uses Twitter only to talk about insignificant things no one cares about, like what they had for breakfast or their latest press release.*

You're reading this book, so obviously you consider yourself someone who "gets it"—that is, understands the importance of social media and wants to know how to best use it within various platforms. Over the years of my very active social media use – and one of the prime reasons I decided to write this book – is how I both love the wit and language of definitions like those above. At the same time, I find it objectionable that in using this wit and uniqueness, users of social media separate themselves too much from others: We get it, we're hip, we use words only those in the know understand.

That sort of separateness reminds me of high school, and the behavior of some people online reminds me of high school-- immature, self-absorbed and adolescent.

Users of Twitter have set up a code of their own. And those who break it might be subjects to "twinsults" like the two definitions above. Like many of the social media sites, Twitter's rules of behavior are self-governing. But here are some of my thoughts for proper use that won't irritate users and will serve you well in the Twitter community.

1.) Choose as short a username as possible to help others retweet your message.

2.) Follow other people (judiciously). This is a basic premise, but nothing demonstrates more that you are a twanker than following no one back. If you can, try to make it more than just 10 people. Conversely, though, there is no social obligation to follow everyone who follows you.

3.) Retweet as often as possible and always leave enough room for retweets (that's the point after all, isn't it?).

4.) In order to make the Twitter platform engaging, allow and respond to direct messages as much as you possibly can.

Instagram: I read one comment about using Instagram that stuck with me for months. Not just because I found it applicable to Instagram, but because I found it applicable to all the social media: *Just because you can, doesn't mean you should*. Everyone's life is interesting, for sure, but sometimes only to themselves. Don't bore people with the minutia of your daily existence. It goes back to my earlier comments about being mindful. Maybe, just maybe, a fair amount of your social media contacts just aren't that interested in the fact that you left your wallet on the kitchen counter this morning and almost ran out of gas.

"SHARE QUALITY NEWS, NOT QUANTITY."

Another comment I found apt, though it was specific to Instagram, is that just because people might be following you on a certain topic, it doesn't mean they are your best friend or even interested in other things you might have to say.

One commenter on Instagram rules in a recent online group wrote it best: Keep your clothes on; be respectful; don't spam; have fun.

Reddit: Here's a forum that bills itself as both open and advocating free speech. So it shouldn't have rules, right? Wrong. It doesn't have many, but it still requires that you don't spam, don't ask for voters or engage in vote manipulation, don't post personal information, and don't post child pornography or sexually suggestive content featuring minors.

There are specific Reddit rules, but again, in trying to

find some common factors in proper social media behaviors, I find some of the following comments I pulled from various forums interesting. When talking to someone online you might want to ask if you'd say the same thing to someone if he or she were sitting in front of you instead of on a computer screen. In other words, stick to the same behavior you would in real life.

I like that concept and think that it should be a universal ruling for all social media. In fact, many sites are now considering disallowing comments from individuals who don't make their identities clear, which effectively eliminates internet trolls.

Other sites are allowing users to maintain an anonymous profile, but are now moderating the types of comments that will be allowed. For instance, the founder of FARK, Drew Curtis, initiated a ban on comments containing misogyny, and has moderators that review the comment sections and remove violating comments. He said, "If the Internet was a dude, we'd all agree that dude has a serious problem with women."

Curtis was met with immediate backlash from the social media, stating that this sort of thing was impossible, but he insisted that "rape jokes," calling "women as a group 'whores' or 'sluts' or similar demeaning terminology," and "jokes suggesting that a woman who suffered a crime was somehow asking for it" would not be tolerated in the FARK forums, which are rife with sarcasm. Racism and "LGBT bashing" were also cited as off-limits. With the announcement of this bold move, Curtis noted, "This represents enough of a departure from pretty much how every other large internet community operates that I figure an announcement is necessary."

I believe that Mr. Curtis' actions are laudable, and should apply in general to other social media sites, in addition to the following: Don't engage in illegal activity; don't post someone's personal information; don't repost stuff that has already been deleted (there was a reason for that); and don't take sides until you understand the topic and the various posters' inclinations and motivations.

Rules evolve. Evolve with them, keeping in mind that when all else fails and you don't know the rules, treat someone the way you would like to be treated.

V. The Professional: Social Media for Business

"How can you squander even one more day not taking advantage of the greatest shifts of our generation? How dare you settle for less when the world has made it so easy for you to be remarkable?" — **Seth Godin**

*I need help creating Facebook, Instagram, and Twitter posts that grab people's attention and help increase my business I need pictures and wording that grab people's attention, and increase likes, comments, and shares -- all fitness based. Looking for an edge.—**from an online ad***

Social media is big business. Countless news outlets reported that Snapchat rejected a $3 billion cash offer from Facebook, holding out for a larger bid or an investment in the company, according to a report that cited unnamed sources.

The Wall Street Journal wrote that the messaging service was entertaining a $200 million investment led by Tencent Holdings, a Chinese e-commerce company. The investment would value Snapchat at $4 billion, the *Journal* reported.

That was, according to some reports, the second time Snapchat has spurned Facebook. The social network offered to acquire Snapchat for more than $1 billion late in 2012. After it was turned down, Facebook released an app to rival Snapchat, but the app had not caught on and trailed far behind Snapchat in users. Facebook then demanded that should their users want to access their Facebook messages on their mobile devices, then they must install Facebook Messenger. This was a move that many Facebook users made without hesitation, but other users revolted and refused to allow Facebook to access their messages separately from their Facebook account.

The amount of money involved in the attempt to purchase Snapchat and then spent in the creation of Facebook Messenger is just one example instance of the limitless budget of social media. That's the social media business, and it's the new reality.

Social media has become so prevalent in our lives, so ubiquitous, that much like steady streams of traffic or background music, we often don't even know they are out there. They exist and are so interwoven in our lives that we don't consciously even think about them. But that thought paradigm must change when social media is used for business purposes.

The professional use of social media is what I want to discuss in this chapter, not the social media *business*, but the *business* of social media. Is it OK to joke around on LinkedIn?

Is it perfectly fine to blather on Facebook that you're actually at work but wasting time posting pictures from a weekend party? The answer to both these question is an emphatic "no."

Even Randi Zuckerberg, sister of Facebook founder Steve Zuckerberg, underestimated how powerful social media is – in her case, Twitter. Who would have expected that? In a recent book, she recalled how she got into trouble for tweeting some nasty comments about a bouncer who wouldn't let her into a bar. "I had no idea the Internet could propel my single tweet so far." *Hmmm. Really*? If she doesn't know the full power of social media, how are the rest of us to gauge how to use social media to help our businesses?

Perhaps studying Randi Zuckerberg's additional comments can shine some light onto that topic. She noted, "I'm a marketer, and sometimes I almost can't take it out of my life. I've had friends call me and say, 'Your life looks so amazing.' And I tell them, 'I'm a marketer; I'm only posting the moments that are amazing.' " The world of social media makes it increasingly difficult to differentiate "real life" from online life. But there is much more to it than that.

To reach the enormous value that social media can provide to a business, it has to prove its worth as a powerful tool to those who are using it to improve, connect, polish, and expand their own business ventures.

And that is the business of social media.

A recent advertisement posted is one tiny example of how vital —how extremely useful and necessary— social media has become in day-to-day business exchanges. In fact, if someone saw this ad three years ago, they likely would not have understood one word of it:

Social Media Community Manager

Are you a digital savvy recent grad with work experience in social media? The McIntyre Group is seeking a Social Media Community Manager. The Community Manager will be responsible for all social media communities, communications and content creation, as well as incorporating online tools and person-to-person networking to create relationships and build the online brand.

Responsibilities:

- Create, manage and grow the company's presence through Facebook, Twitter, Vine, Instagram and other strategically relevant online arenas

- Create strategic marketing/communications plans to provide direction for the company's public-facing communications

- Write material for social media channels which can include Facebook, Twitter, Vine, and Instagram

- Support customers by answering questions however they come in (Facebook/Twitter) and manage any online feedback forums

- Offer continual commentary to show community support on all social media forums

- Be able to provide feedback with a positive voice—even in negative situations

- Use measurement tools to provide reports on metrics, and continually find ways to improve on those metrics through testing and new initiatives

Requirements:

- Experience managing Online Communities and familiarity with Facebook, Twitter and other social media outlets
- A Bachelor's Degree in Business, Journalism or related field
- The ability to create well written blog posts, new content, and posts in a timely manner with little to no supervision
- Excellent writing and proofreading skills

That's a lot of requirements and responsibility for what appears to be an entry-level job. And it speaks volumes as to how business views the importance of the social media. Gone are the days—if anyone can actually remember them—when you went about your business of business and hoped your marketing department knew what it was doing to sell you, your company, your brand and your name.

The point is, today, whether you are an entrepreneur trying to grab a tiny hold within a vast and competitive new market, or you're representing an established business stuck in the past—doing things as they were done five years ago—you need to boost your business using blogs, social networking sites, multimedia, and online review sites.

How? Are there rules? Of course there are. We all need help. The three excerpts from various media demonstrate the pervasive and all-encompassing need to not only be aware of social media for business, but to know how to use it effectively.

I can cite my own professional ventures as an example of how important social media has become. I spend a majority of my time between my homes in the Middle East and the United States. Given my rigorous travel schedule, I spend a lot of time on planes, while running a business with global implications and reach. I need to get in touch with people all over the world on a daily basis, and like most people in business, I usually need to do it *yesterday*!

I would not stand much of a chance among the lion's den of my competitors if I entrusted my business ideas to the more static media, sending out letters and leaving phone messages. How important has the social media become for business? One has only to look at the help-wanted ad above.

Consider this: I know a publisher that won't even consider a book if the author doesn't have a website or social media accounts. The days of the author recluses like Salinger and Hemingway seem to have vanished in this modern society.

How much do you know about what social media is out there for your professional use? How much of it do you use? How do you use it? Have you considered employing an expert in this ever-evolving and vitally important field?

A remarkable new industry has sprung from the fact that few people actually know how to use the social media in business. It's no wonder that these companies, many of which call themselves simply "social media consultants," offer training, workshops and specialized advice to help business owners navigate through the maze that social media has become. One company states: "Let XXXXX Marketing [I am protecting their identity here] help in the training of your staff on how to best utilize the likes of Facebook, Twitter, LinkedIn, Google+, You Tube, and blogging to reach your corporate objectives."

These consultants (and I agree wholeheartedly) assert that many companies lack the experience of working with the various social media platforms, or they are not maximizing how they use social media. Also frequently noted is that many companies don't possess a strategy for using social media to improve their business.

LinkedIn, Facebook, Twitter, YouTube, blogs and other social media are (or can be) extremely powerful marketing tools. Do you need a consultant to tell you that? I don't think so. Do you need a consultant to help you get your message across the various social media platforms? Most likely, yes. Social media is now a full-time job, given the global nature of it. Employing the skills of a professional can assist your business in managing your public persona.

When considering hiring someone to assist you with your social media plans, I ask you to consider once again my request that you adopt a philosophy of mindfulness—of understanding who you are trying to reach, and developing a thoughtful, polite, and insightful strategy that first considers the medium you are using.

Do you intend to employ the more conservative and rigid LinkedIn platform, or do you prefer the more casual environment of Facebook? You should also ask yourself who you are trying to reach.

Do you want to connect with the stiff and formal CEO of a corporation you'd like to partner with, or are you trying to get in touch with some laid back friends who have some money to invest? Then consider the fact that your social media messages need to be consistently engaging and updated in order to keep or gain market share within your niche.

Understanding those parameters means that you're halfway there, or maybe even further.

There are rules, of course, and then there are *rules*. Where is the line between being inappropriate or rude, and being illegal? What if you're a chief executive and you want to tweet about a new purchase that will increase the price of your stock exponentially? Stockholders, of course, would love to hear about that and buy more stock. But is that legal? Or is that insider trading?

The Securities and Exchange Commission ruled recently that chief executives can now feel free to post, blog or tweet — as long as they inform investors about their social media strategy first, and outlined new disclosure rules that clarify how companies can use Facebook, Twitter and other social networks to disseminate information, provided they meet certain requirements.

Granted, not too many of us are CEOs, but I wanted to point that out as a way of showing how potentially powerful the social media are—and how misuse can create legal problems, if not simply irritate users.

Let's take a look at how some of the corporate biggies advise their employees. Keep in mind one very important thing as you read these guidelines: while the sampling below is relatively small, it speaks large volumes regarding the usage of courtesy and common sense.

IBM

Don't pick fights, be the first to correct your own mistakes, and don't alter previous posts without indicating that you have done so.

Try to add value. Provide worthwhile information and perspective. IBM's brand is best represented by its people and what you publish may reflect on IBM's brand.

Speak in the first person. Use your own voice. Bring your own personality to the forefront. Say what is on your mind.

BBC

With conversations, participate online. Don't "broadcast" messages to users.

With moderation, only police where we have to. Trust our users where we don't.

Tone of voice. We should be sensitive to the expectations of existing users of the specific site. If we add a BBC presence, we are joining their site rather than the opposite. Users are likely to feel that they already have a significant stake in it. When adding an informal BBC presence, we should "go with the grain" and be sensitive to user customs and conventions to avoid giving the impression that the BBC is imposing itself on them and their space.

Intel

Always pause and think before posting. That said, reply to comments in a timely manner, when a response is appropriate. But if it gives you pause, pause. If you're about to publish something that makes you even the slightest bit uncomfortable, don't shrug it off and hit 'send.' Take a minute to review these guidelines and try to figure out what's bothering you, then fix it. If you're still unsure, you might want to discuss it with your manager or legal representative. Ultimately, what you publish is yours - as is the responsibility. So be sure.

Perception is reality. In online social networks, the lines between public and private, personal and professional are blurred. Just by identifying yourself as an Intel employee, you are creating perceptions about your expertise and about Intel by our shareholders, customers, and the general public-and perceptions about you by your colleagues and managers. Do us all proud. Be sure that all content associated with you is consistent with your work and with Intel's values and professional standards.

It's a conversation. Talk to your readers like you would talk to real people in professional situations. In other words, avoid overly pedantic or "composed" language. Don't be afraid to bring in your own personality and say what's on your mind. Consider content that's open-ended and invites response. Encourage comments.

KODAK

Be external. You don't have to be 100% internally focused. Link to other blogs, videos, and news articles. Retweet what others have to say.

Post frequently. It's a lot of work, but don't post to your blog then leave it for two weeks. Readers won't have a reason to follow you on Twitter or check your blog if they can't expect new content regularly.

Be careful when sharing information about yourself or others.

SAP

Separate opinions from facts, and make sure your audience can see the difference. Be engaged and be informed. Read the contributions of others. Know what the current conversations are and what people are saying in order to see if, and how, you may be able to contribute a new perspective. Participation is the fuel of social computing. Aim for quality, not quantity.

Offer your contribution with context whenever you can. Provide links to other blogs, media articles or whatever sources you think are necessary. Make your content rich and interesting for others to read. Consider attaching documents when necessary (but not SAP internal documents, confidential or not, of course!). And in every case, keep the language simple and flowing. If you start a blog, encourage feedback and conversation - make sure your readers can add feedback to your blog and respond in a timely manner. A two-way exchange allows for a more meaningful conversation.

ZAPPOS

Be real and use your best judgement.

So what does this all mean? What are the rules? Let's distill them into their purest form so you can go out into the world and start selling yourself and your business without upsetting people.

Make producing quality content your first and most pressing priority. You wouldn't go a meeting with a new and potentially lucrative partner wearing pajamas. Your writing, your posts and your promotions will say a lot about you and your company. Be clear, be concise, be accurate, be witty, and be creative.

What you say on social media is probably even more important than a real-life face-to-face meeting because you are speaking to a larger audience.

Be open, frank and truthful. If you're not, eventually people will know. Remember that social media is a conversation that goes both ways. Producing wonderfully witty and clear content is only one side of the conversation – your side. Remember that the other half of the game is listening to what your customers – the people you are tweeting or Facebooking or Linking-In – are saying to you.

Focus, focus, focus. Because social media has grown so large, many users have drifted into smaller communities that share common interests. If you are just starting up a business or are trying to establish a brand, find these smaller communities. It will save plenty of precious time trying to reach the right people—and it will stop you from wasting time pitching idea to an ocean full of uninterested readers. Over time, with a consistent message, your brand will build a loyal and engaged base.

Finally, remember that you can build your business using social media and that you can build your social media using your business. It's a two-way street. Business owners often view social media as a component of marketing or PR. However, social media is also a great way to build rapport as a leader in the space you are operating within.

VI. Leader or Wallflower: Which One Are You?

Given my multicultural background and my comfort and pleasure in adapting to wherever I happen to be at the moment, I'm at ease adjusting within nearly any culture. I'm just as comfortable taking a one-dirham *abra* ride across the beautiful Dubai Creek at sunset as I am shopping at Faneuil Hall Marketplace in Boston. I was recently intrigued by a lecture I heard by writer Pico Iyer. "What do you say when people ask where you come from?" he asked. That fascinated me. Iyer, Indian by blood and ethnicity, pointed out the he had actually never set foot in India. Was he English by virtue of his education? American by the many years he spent there and where his parents lived? Or was he from Japan, the place that he most closely relates to within his deepest psyche?

Iyer's discussion was more of a meditation than a lecture. What he said appealed to me not simply because it resonated with my own life, but because it got me thinking about the separate places we make for ourselves in the social media.

What is your sense of place in the social media? Are you a leader? Or are you a wallflower?

Where he comes from, Iyer said, is more a matter of soul than soil. I think that is true also of where you are—where people perceive you are—on social media.

From that simple message, I started thinking about how different people use, and at times abuse, the wonderful potential of social media; how they claim different territories, assert themselves (and perhaps *insert* themselves), and how others view them.

As I pointed out in Chapter III, "You Are What You Post," people on social media take on different personalities.

My simple advice here is to be yourself, be true to your ideals, and don't assume an online personality that is not you. But it is not necessarily that simple.

Whether you are on Facebook, Twitter, Instagram, email, LinkedIn, SnapChat, YouTube, or any of the many other social media options, are you perceived as a wallflower or a leader? Do you come across as honest, or not to be believed? Are you someone who attracts viewers and readers, or someone who repels them?

Let's take the online personalities concept one step further and refine it a bit. How do other see you? Do you seem like a witty, talented, and knowledgeable person with whom they can't wait to engage? Or do you come across as someone who is shut down immediately?

There are ways to assure yourself a place in either category.

Of course, the winning tag is a better thing to be graced with. But take a look at both. Regardless of your choice of social media platform, it is important to ask if you use social media to enhance your work, perhaps your recreation with such things as traveling, studying, or spending time with friends. Before we get into the concept of winning and losing, let's take a look at some various brain-types and how they perceive and use social media. Maybe you can see yourself in one of these three types of people.

Ask yourself this: In person, do you almost automatically attract people? Do you seem to draw them to you much like a magnet attracts metal? Have you a large circle of friends? I think those qualities would allow you to easily attract and interact with people when you use media like Facebook, Twitter, or even LinkedIn.

Maybe you see yourself as a geek. (Hey, geek is the new cool.) An analytical sort who understands the technicalities and the importance of the emotional aspects of building an audience. You understand completely how social media works in terms of clicks, pastes, and sends. You're not challenged by the tools of social media, but you're not as confident in a "social" sense as to how to best convey your message in order to allow you to build your business and groups of followers.

Perhaps you see yourself as a natural storyteller. The kind of person who can write a post or a tweet that compels people to stop in their tracks, drop whatever they're doing and read and share your words. Do the poets weep when swept away by your beautiful prose and quick wit? That's good, because we have to look at all social media as the ability to tell a story. If you can do that, you're ahead of many when it comes to best utilizing social media for your professional self.

The three brain types above have many advantages when it comes to social media.   But let's be realistic, most of us don't fit squarely into those categories. Most of us maybe lurk a bit on Facebook, or tweet occasionally or add something new to our LinkedIn profile, or start a blog that somehow ends up going nowhere, but we really don't know what we're doing and haven't really thought much about how to make the best use of social media for our personal and business growth.

I truly believe that by understanding your personality type, you can make an informed choice about how you represent yourself on social media, or how you want those who work for you to represent you.

Understanding your personality—which I swear is not that tough to do—will positively impact the way you respond to different situations during your social media interactions.

I'm not talking about faking a new personality. I'm talking about actually becoming aware of your personality and using that knowledge to become social media savvy.

Whatever you do, don't say, "But I'm an introvert and I cannot adapt to social situations." When you are managing your social media situations, you want to seek out and share your ideas with an audience that identifies with you and your brand; ideally as your business grows, the larger the audience the better. Remind yourself that you have something worthwhile to share and simply do it. If you're an introvert, or think you're an introvert, remember that if that's true, you prefer quality over quantity. Well, guess what? That's perfect for a Facebook post or a tweet. Keep it short and sweet and to the point. It doesn't matter if ten people are reading or 10,000. If you can accept that, you are on your way to being a social media winner.

Another commonly cited example of introverts: "I hate being the center of attention." That doesn't matter either, because once you make a winning and insightful post on any social media, the post itself will become the center of attention, not you. Get it? It's about social media, not you. Using social media in this fashion makes you a winner from the outset.

A social media leader needs to be a producer of interesting and compelling information, a calm distributor of that information, and to be seen as someone to turn to for reasoned (can we say wise?) advice.

I can absolutely guarantee that you will be seen as a social media leader if you take a deep breath and think about where you want to go. Be thoughtful and think about these following things:

Find communities that respect you and you will naturally grow as well.

Once you are in the midst of like-minded and knowledgeable people, take an interest in what they are saying, too. It's not a one-way street. If you show others in your network that you appreciate what they are tweeting or posting, they will take in interest in you as well. Another way of looking at it is this: If you want people to do things for you, do something for them.

Remember that social media has the potential to speed up human interactions. So being interested in what others have to say and promoting their interest can produce amazing results for you very quickly.

If you want to be a leader in your social media community, whatever that may be, try helping other users in other communities. How's that for a concept? Being helpful and kind and thoughtful can improve your image. As I might have mentioned before, it's really a matter of common sense.

But while you're doing that, it's important to keep in mind that you need to concentrate on the users and readers and community companions who can be valuable to your mission, whatever that might be. Ask yourself these four questions: Does it build reputation? Does it deliver value to me or someone else? Does it increase connectedness to my community? Is it efficient?

Basically, it comes down to this: As you build your reputation as a leader, your reputation will begin to take on a life of its own.

VII. Elegance, Eloquence and Expression

"RU OK? LOL!! TTYL."

or

"I'm worried about you, and concerned enough that I'd like to speak with you today."

There are two schools of thought about communicating using the various social media. Do you simply blast it out, using accepted abbreviations and shortcuts, paying little if any attention to proper spelling, punctuation or organization? Or do you take the time to write something that meets generally accepted standards of writing?

The first school is based on this concept: The rapidity and importance of sending as many messages as possible in as short a time as possible – and the ease at which one can do this on dozens of social media – has led to an epidemic of abysmal grammar, poor spelling, nonexistent punctuation, and the loss of generations of education. This style has writing teachers and professors worldwide standing by to revolt.

The second school is based on this concept: The rapidity and importance of sending as many messages as possible in as short a time as possible—and the ease at which one can do this on dozens of social media--had led to a wave of creativity and function that has never before been seen since writers first put pen ever so slowly to paper. In the heart of the digital age, the concept of writing, especially to young adults, seems antiquated. Having grown up with laptops and iPads, many of them struggle to remember the last time they sat down with pen and paper.

Confusing, isn't it?

What I would like to discuss in this chapter is a blending of these two schools—something we can call the Netiquette Academy. And that, dear readers, says that you should take advantage of the absolutely tremendous opportunities offered by the social media to be stunningly creative and voluminous in your writing. But—and this is most important—you should do so following generally accepted standards of proper writing, spelling, punctuation, and grammar.

The moral of the story: bad grammar not only hinders your social media efforts, but it has the ability to thwart any credibility or authority you may have in your respective field. Writing poorly reflects poorly upon you. You should consider not only what your social media posts say, but also how they reflect your grammatical skills. Let's face it, an incredible amount of incorrect punctuation, spelling mistakes and bad grammar has crept into blogs, posts and tweets all over the web, leading to a nearly new language.

Some writing advocates state that Twitter's frugal word structure, Facebook's short-post style, and the use of abbreviations in texting are eroding basic writing skills. I recently came across this comment from a Florida college professor who was running a summer camp for aspiring writers.

"I asked my students to write four lines of dialogue they had over the weekend," he said. "Three of them reached for their phones to read their text messages. They said they couldn't remember any face-to-face conversations."

That is scary to me, but it also demonstrates how prevalent our use of social media has become.

A recent report published by Clarion University in Pennsylvania shows social media and text messages are "consistently associated with the use of particularly informal written communication techniques, along with formatting problems, nonstandard orthography, and grammatical errors." Ironically, that poorly written and confusing statement points out one thing: social media can lead to poor writing in general.

Social media has opened up the doors of communication as wide as they can go and now they provide limitless opportunity for people to connect both personally and in business. But having the doors open all of the time does have a downside; all this freedom to communicate leaves you exposed to the elements of the weather-in this case, displaying poor writing or grammatical skills.

Don't let your readers think you somehow left school in the third grade on your way to Facebook and Twitter.

Even the most disciplined grammatical expert will likely experience a typo when using social media, and there will always be points of grammar to quibble about in any form of writing. The goal of proper grammar is to eliminate any distractions from your message, making your point clear so that people can get to the heart of what you're trying to communicate.

Personally, I think that if someone in business consistently showcases bad grammar or a professional constantly posts information rife with errors, it can reflect poorly upon them. True, you might be able to delete a post after you realize you messed up "its" and "it's," but if that post has been retweeted or shared or promoted by others in any way, it's ultimately permanent and your grammatical error will stay alive and well in cyberspace forever.

We will talk in this chapter about some of the things NOT to do, but also provide you with plenty of options of things TO DO that will polish your image. What we want really is *e-legance, e-loquence and e-xpression.*

If I could distill my own thoughts into just one vibrant and concentrated sentence, it would be this: Respecting language earns respect on social media.

Things have evolved so quickly in the world of social media – something that a dozen years ago barely existed – it is hard to speak of traditional web writing and composition. It wasn't so long ago that being an online writer was a cutting-edge career. Bloggers and others found themselves the new kids on the block and at times actually looked down on writers from the various print media. As we all well know, the only thing that is constant is change. And online things have been changing very quickly.

Remember now that in today's social media you are writing for and to *people*, not search engines. Writing for people takes a real shift in attitude and skill. Use variety in your writing, and think of it as having a vibrant conversation to engage your audience with an irresistible variety of short-form entries. The people you are writing for should read a compelling array of entries that inform, engage, and entertain. The best Twitter streams and Facebook walls include a degree of one-on-one conversation. As a writer, this means you need to make a shift in your mind. Instead of writing at an audience, you are having to engage in a one-on-one conversation.

A website or blog is often the first place that you go to learn a little bit more about the individual who is posting it. So if your online content has many spelling errors or grammatical mistakes, then why should your visitors take you seriously?

Now add in the spelling mistakes in your tweets and updates, and suddenly you look less professional or even uneducated.

And not to sound haughty about grammar, because there is nothing more unlikeable in my view than a prim and officious grammarian (you know they type, they correct your speech before you are even finished talking) but there is a simply unbelievable amount of unintelligible writing out there on public display—and I'm not just talking about abbreviated words that are made to fit into Twitter updates.

Think of the goal of your social media posts first, and much of your potential problem will disappear, I have found. Who are you writing for? And what do you want them to learn? There is much elegance in simplicity, brevity and clarity. If you keep your story, post or message simple—without trying to cram too much in and without developing too many digressive threads—you have a much better chance of engaging your readers and keeping them interested. You don't have to tell them everything in one message. Less is more.

Always, always, remember to respect your readers. Think before you write. Assess what are you actually trying to convey and how will the reader react. Sarcasm or irony might be easy to pull off in a conversation, but even the most proficient sarcasm user admits that it is eminently more difficult to make clear sarcasm in writing. There is no sarcasm font.

Despite the instantaneous nature of social media, always resist the urge to dash something off in a flash. I know that it is so very easy to do, but restrain yourself and put some thought into your writing. It will pay off for you much better in the end. Consider your reader.

I heartily believe that social media in many ways makes us better story tellers. It forces us to learn how to better explain something and places us in positions where we more often must try to persuade someone about something. Ultimately, that makes us better writers. Regardless of the media, I think good writing is more important than ever.

On a practical level, I've learned a few simple processes that will make your posts resonate with authority, if for no other reason than that your readers are not distracted by glaring grammatical mistakes and types of silliness.

- Before posting, read what you've written out loud, slowly and clearly. Mistakes will jump out, trust me.

- If you have time—and you should make the time—have someone else read what you've written.

- Do not, under any circumstances, rely on spellcheck.

Follow these simple rules:

1. **Affect vs. effect**. The easiest way to remember the difference between the two is affect means "to influence." So if you're going to influence something, you will have an affect. If it's the result of something, it's an effect.

2. **Commas, in general**. Slow down when you're writing and read your copy out loud. You don't want to make this mistake: Let's eat grandma vs. let's eat, grandma. Poor grandma will be eaten if you forget the comma.

3. **Their, they're, and there**. You'd think everyone learned this rule in fourth grade, but it's a very common mistake. Use "there" when referring to a location, "their" to indication possession, and "they're" when you mean to say "they are."

4. **Care less**. The dismissive "I could care less" you hear all the time is incorrect. If you could care less, that means there is more you could care less about the topic. Most people omit the "not" in that phrase. It should be, "I couldn't care less."

5. **Irregardless**. This word doesn't exist. It's regardless.

6. **Your and you're**. Another mistake you see in people's social media profiles and in the content they create is not correctly using "your" and "you're." If you're meaning to say "you are," the correct word is "you're" (like at the beginning of this sentence). Otherwise the word is "your."

7. **Fewer vs. less**. Another common mistake, "less" refers to quantity and "fewer" to a number. For instance, Facebook has fewer than 5,000 employees.

8. **Quotation marks**. Among great debate, people ask all the time whether or not punctuation belongs inside or outside quotation marks. It belongs inside.

9. **More than vs. over**. I'm pretty sure the advertising agency created this grammatical error. Instead of saying, "We had more than 50 percent growth" in ad copy, "over" allows for more space. So they say, "We had over 50 percent growth."

10. **Me vs. I**. I was reading something written by a big muckety-muck the other day and the copy read, "This year has brought a big personal development for my wife and I…" No, no, no! If you were going to say that without the mention of your wife, you wouldn't say, "This year has brought a big personal development for I." You would say "me." So this year has brought a big personal development for my wife and me.

11. **You bring to, and take from.**

12. **Unique.** This cannot be qualified. Something is unique or it is not. It is never *really* unique or *sort of* unique.

There are many useful and excellent grammar usage books. My favorite, for its clarity, brevity, and accuracy is *Elements of Style*.

On a more long-rage basis with an eye toward becoming a good writer—and I think all users of social media should aspire to this—take a long approach. Any skill needs to be developed. Think about the following:

Writing is no different from many other skills. You need to gain experience before you can reach a certain level of fluency, of comfort in expressing yourself. It doesn't happen overnight. One of the first rules of writing is to avoid clichés.

But I'm going to ignore that and say this: Practice makes perfect. Get into the habit of writing every single day. Write often enough so that writing becomes second nature.

Let's face it here. I am stating the obvious: Learn the rules of basic grammar. If grammatical rules are not followed, your writing will be very difficult to understand and follow. Grammar provides the building blocks of language, therefore a missing comma or a misplaced period will change the flow of an article.

Mark Twain once wrote to a friend: "I'm sorry this letter is so long. If I had more time it would have been much shorter." Good advice. Do not fall into the trap of believing that longer articles are always better. There is no point saying something in one thousand words if it can be said in one hundred. When you want to say something meaningful, be concise and get straight to the point.

Most excellent writers are avid and rabid readers. You can learn a lot about your craft by reading regularly. Pay attention to what other writers do, how they do it, and why they do it. Read as many books by other authors on subjects that you might be writing about as you can. You will subconsciously pick up an eye for writing styles and an ear for new words.

Write, write, write. Research, research, research. Every topic you cover should be researched thoroughly. This will improve the quality of your content and ensure that the arguments you put forward are strong.

VIII. TWITTER

Twitter is powerful. Twitter is easy to use. Twitter is popular beyond belief, used daily by hundreds of millions of users, by some estimates.

Twitter was originally an internal service for employees of Odeo, but it became public in 2006, and by the following year it began to grow astronomically. Though still far short of Facebook as the most popular form of social media, Twitter continues to grow daily. And as it does, its influence expands and so does the need for understanding its oddities and the need for polite discourse.

For all those reasons, it is a social medium that is an absolutely ripe tool for reaching as many people as you possibly can for all the right reasons—sharing information, opinions, and breaking news, to name just a few. And for all those reasons, it is equally as ripe to allow you to embarrass yourself beyond belief. Get the wrong Twitter reputation, and you might soon be longing for the day when people communicated by writing letters, mailing them, and hoping to get a response in a week or two.

Take just two examples of the power of the Tweet:

The New York City Police Department, in what I would guess was a moment of shortsightedness, tweeted that it would like users to share photos of their interactions with New York's Finest, as they call themselves. The idea was to have thousands of New Yorkers tweet photos of themselves being helped by police officers or perhaps being rescued in a time of peril or in the middle of a hug of thanks for some valiant police effort.

What they got instead, which much to their chagrin went out over the Twitter universe, were hundreds of tweets showing various people being beaten or handcuffed or pepper sprayed by the men in blue.

What was meant to be a public relations coup of some sort turned into an act of public defiance; Twitter provides a setting that allows users to demonstrate how they genuinely feel about issues, and in this case, they stated their strong opinions and experiences regarding police brutality rather than police assistance.

Another unfortunate Twitter mishap from American car manufacturer Chrysler occurred when a rogue employee gained access to the company's official twitter stream. Whether that employee thought he was joking, or was simply disgruntled, or thought perhaps that his bit of misguided wit would be seen by only a few friends—he was deeply mistaken. Millions of people saw it.

Their Twitter page is usually a place where visitors can find such innocuous tweets as "Hope everyone has a great #MoparMonday" and "Just 17 days away from #SF6 and we're pumped!" What surprised followers found one day was the following observation: "I find it ironic that Detroit is known as the #motorcity and yet no one here knows how to fucking drive."

Chrysler, in a flurry of embarrassed investigations, hastily removed the tweet and apologized, only later to discover that the tweet had come not from a Chrysler employee, but from an employee of the media service it had hired to tweet. The moral of the story? Take your tweets seriously.

Another example of both the power of Twitter and the need to take it seriously occurred this year in Turkey, when its prime minister, Recep Tayyip Erdogan, vowed to "eradicate" Twitter, then shut it and several other social media avenues down—including YouTube.

Within one hour, public outrage was evident—which

once again shows the incredible power of the social media to influence political outcomes. With social media such as Twitter available, governments can no longer control information.

But they apparently keep trying.

In Turkey after the prime minister's comments, Twitter hashtags like #TwitterisblockedinTurkey," "#DictatorErdogan" and "TurkeyBlockedTwitter" surged to the service's top worldwide trends.

The prime minister's almost arrogant disbelief in the power of Twitter was clear when he said of his plan to shut it down, "The international community will say this and that, and it doesn't concern me one bit. They will see the power of the Turkish Republic. "

Using a new law in which he sought to silence any opposition or dissent, the prime minister had the authority to close any website offering opinions different from his ruling party in a matter of hours. Two opposition leaders each had thousands of followers. And with upcoming elections, the easiest way to eliminate differing opinions was to erase them from public discussion.

That is the power of Twitter—an almost backhanded compliment of its power and its popularity—based, unfortunately, on fear.

So why is Twitter so popular and so powerful? Why is it so capable of instilling fear in people who are afraid of having so much information available to be read by so many?

In our modern multicultural world, someone with even a basic idea of how to tweet can track hundreds of things quickly. It really is ideal for a world in which many of us suffer from very short attention spans. In fact, a recent study claims that human beings now have shorter attention spans than goldfish. We want things quickly, we want them clearly, and we want them now. With its size limit of no more than 140 characters per tweet, this format is perfect for our short attention spans. This size restriction has made Twitter popular because it forces the user to use clever language in order to convey a message succinctly.

Whether you are tweeting for business, for fun, for education, news or instant information, Twitter is truly wide open, perhaps more so than any other social media. The real point is, it's not just for young tech-savvy kids; it's for everyone, as a growing number of politicians, celebrities, and sports stars join every day. US vice president Joe Biden, who is no stranger to putting his foot in his mouth when he speaks, nonetheless tweets.

Movie star Robert Downey Jr. joined the twitterverse this year. He created a self-assured bio reading, "You know who I am." His first tweet, was a photo of the *Iron Man* star holding a sign that read, "Talk to me, Twitter." Former National Basketball Association star Shaquille O'Neal has developed an ardent Twitter following because of tweets like this: Shaq (@The Real_Shaq) Yo momma so old she owes Moses a dollar.

Twitter is great for quite a few things, and allows you to follow people and situations as if you are right beside or within them. Twitter has actually produced the term "microblogging." It is micro, certainly, since you can't go over 140 characters, but it is blogging because you can write about anything.

With Twitter you can ask quick questions and getting quick answers. What is the capital of Connecticut? Has anyone eaten at the new Indian place on 44th Street? If you don't have too many followers, you can avail yourself of such websites as Mahalo by sending a question to @answers.

You can keep up with the news on Twitter as well. All of the traditional media outlets have Twitter accounts, from newspapers to magazines to TV stations and cable news. Don't care about the news? You can use Twitter to arrange a dinner with friends.

Twitter can also serve as an outlet to vent your anger over anything from your favorite team's poor play to a remark you heard on TV or on the subway coming home to a lousy waitress or a noisy neighbor. Letting it out on Twitter instead of taking it out on your dog or someone at work has its advantages, but be careful. You can get into trouble if you are too quick with your Twitter trigger fingers. You don't want to get a Twitter reputation for constant complaining, and nobody wants to follow someone who only uses Twitter to complain.

If you are into sports, Twitter has a search feature that allows you to keep up on the latest information. There is an astounding number of players who tweet, so you can not only get media reports, but also the latest inside scoop on what is going on with the team. As an added benefit, many of the tweets from players and insiders are often quite funny.

Interested in politics? Barack Obama and Joe Biden both tweet. They use Twitter to express their viewpoints and to reach constituents in a way that is not filtered by newspaper and television reports. I'm not sure if this is good or bad, since there is no balance, but if you love politics, Twitter is a great way to follow the latest and to respond in kind if you want.

Want an even more powerful illustration of the power of Twitter? Pope Francis joined the twitterverse in 2013, and followers can follow him on @Pontifex. I can say no more.

Let's face it, Twitter is a great way – an absolutely terrific way – to simply waste time.

We all have a lot of those spare moments during the day, whether it's spacing out in front of your computer at work, staring at a bad TV show, or – to be perfectly frank – sitting on the toilet. Many of us have taken to filling those empty moments by scrolling through our Twitter feeds.

Twitter itself is such a wonderful universe and such a true gift to social media that it would be extremely difficult to point to all the things you can do with it, because you can do just about anything.

Before we get into what I feel are the essentials of proper Twitter use, let's take a look at some basic Twitter terms. I have adapted these wonderful basic definitions from #hashtags.org.

Tweet: The message you post and send out to your followers is called a "tweet." You can also use this word as a verb, as with "tweeting a message." Twitter has limited the length of tweets to under 140 characters, so the best tweets are those that are concise and direct to the point. Also, tweets are on a public domain, so they are searchable.

Follower: A follower is a Twitter user who has subscribed to your account so he or she can see all your posts and updates on your own page. Generally, if you "follow" another user, that user follows you back. This is not symmetrical, however, as that user may also choose not to follow back. The more followers you have, the wider audience your tweets will get and the greater influence you will likely have in the micro-blogging community.

Retweet: Also used as either a noun or a verb, a retweet simply is a sharing of your original post by another user in his or her own page. Some retweet manually by typing "RT@username" before adding comments to the post. The "username" is the original source of the post. A retweet is used when a user thinks that your post is interesting or entertaining enough to share with his or her own followers.

Unfollow: Used as a verb, 'unfollow' happens when one of your followers decides he or she doesn't want to be updated with your posts anymore and gets out of your network.

Mention: To communicate with another Twitter use, you can either send a direct message (privately) or mention the user in your public post so others can also see.

DM: Short for "direct message", the DM is a tweet-like message that is sent privately and can only be seen by the sender and the receiver. You can only send a DM to somebody who is following you. The limit for DMs is still under 140 characters.

Hashtag: A hashtag is a keyword or phrase that is preceded by a pound (#) sign. Anybody who clicks the hashtag will be led to a page that lists all Twitter users who have applied the hashtag in their own posts.

Engagement: When you 'engage' with another user, you are making conversation on the Twitterverse with a string of responses and exchanges.

Feed: A 'feed' is a list of updates or tweets that are constantly being updated. They are usually arranged in chronological order, with the most recently updated ones at the top for easier viewing.

Trend: When a hashtag is particularly popular on Twitter, it becomes a trend or a trending topic. The Twitter homepage presents a list of the most popular hashtags at a certain time. Your homepage also shows a list of trends at the left side, although these trends are tailored according to who you are following.

TWITTER BASIC RULES

There is a lot more to using Twitter than knowing you have only 140 characters in which to express yourself. In many ways, the rules governing how you tweet and retweet are exactly what I have been stressing throughout this book: You are what you tweet. If you are vulgar or appear unintelligent, you tweets will carry that message to the world.

Here is my own rule number one: Do not share anything in public you might regret later. There is absolutely no shortage of embarrassed tweeters – usually celebrities, sports icons, or politicians – making apologies for an intemperate remark, which is then retweeted and picked up by TV and print media and explodes into the daily stream of broadcast news.

First, try to think clearly about what you are doing and what the purpose of your tweet is; 140 characters is not permission to be so terse that no one can understand you.

Think it out, and spell it out. With that in mind, try to keep your tweets longer than one word. No one will know what you are trying to say and many people might be annoyed. It should absolutely go without saying that there is zero room for crassness or boring posts.

You are not tweeting in a vacuum. The Twitterverse is actually a conversation. Try to be a part of it. Just as you wouldn't in a normal face-to-face conversation, don't butt in unless you know what people are talking about. Try to respond only when you think you can add value to the conversation. It is also important to make sure that your profile is filled out as completely as possible, especially as your audience grows. That way people can see who you are and why you might actually have something worthwhile to add.

When you first begin to tweet on a regular basis, start slowly and build. If you start to follow someone, give him or her a chance to check out your profile and your tweets to see if he or she wants to follow you back. That way you can build a loyal base. Get to know your audience and actually get to like them. It will provide a benefit that will continue to grow as your audience continues to grow.

Obviously, you don't want to bore your audience to tears. If you tweet too many accounts of your breakfast menus or workouts at the gym or what you decided to wear today— you won't have much of an audience.

Try to use common sense, of course, and protect yourself by not tweeting or retweeting something you are not sure about. A good rule of thumb is to ask yourself if you would be able to defend you tweet in person.

Accuracy, clarity, brevity, and wit will rule the day. Have fun with those 140 characters and play with them. It's a challenge but also an adventure.